Original title:
Embracing the Spirit of Christmas

Copyright © 2024 Creative Arts Management OÜ
All rights reserved.

Author: Benjamin Caldwell
ISBN HARDBACK: 978-9916-94-030-3
ISBN PAPERBACK: 978-9916-94-031-0

Old Traditions, New Beginnings

The socks are hung with care,
But we forgot the snacks to share.
Santa's list is quite a mess,
Grandma's sweats are now the dress.

Carols sung off-key and loud,
Pet cat thinks he's in a crowd.
Cookies shaped like festive trees,
Even burnt ones can please.

Miracles in the Softest Glow

Twinkling lights on every street,
Watch out, it's a tinsel feat!
Mistletoe with strings of threads,
But I just kissed the guy next door's pets.

Snowflakes fall without a plan,
Wacky snowmen in a clan.
Hot cocoa spilled on the rug,
Oops! That was my Christmas hug.

Warmth That Fills the Air

The fireplace gives a gentle gleam,
But Dad's still lost in holiday dreams.
Burning logs and popcorn strings,
Mom blinds Santa with shiny blings.

Chocolate stains from little hands,
Flying reindeer on ice-bound lands.
Silly hats, the joy they bring,
Fun in every little thing.

Joyous Hearts Uniting

Family photos gone askew,
Silly faces, no one knew.
Awkward hugs and laughter loud,
The whole neighborhood feels so proud.

Games that go awry with cheers,
We laugh, forgetting all our fears.
Baking mishaps fill the air,
With every blunder, love is there.

Celebrations in Every Corner

Snowmen dance in the streets,
With carrot noses, oh so sweet.
Elves are baking, flour fights,
While seniors shop on mulled wine nights.

Santa's reindeer, wild and spry,
Practicing loops in the frosty sky.
Gift-wrapped cats, a purring sight,
Plotting mischief in the night!

The Calm Before the Snowfall

The world is hushed, preparations too,
Anticipation, what will we do?
The cat's in the tree, oh dear, oh no!
Our holiday cheer just stole the show!

Stockings hung with care, we hope,
That dad won't drink all the eggnog, nope!
Frosty's melting—what a tease!
Hot cocoa spills with a sense of ease!

Candles Flickering in the Twilight

Candles flicker, shadows play,
Someone knocked the fruitcake away!
A turkey's burnt, but spirits soar,
As Aunt Edna preps for an encore.

Lights strung wrong, a tangled mess,
Yet laughter reigns, we're blessed, no stress.
As carols echo, off-key and loud,
From the kitchen, oh, we feel so proud!

A Canvas of Kindness

Snowflakes dance like tiny sprites,
Kids with snowballs in epic fights.
The dog joins in, with joyful woofs,
Chasing shadows, raising goofs.

Gifts exchanged with glittery flair,
Grandpa snoozes in his favorite chair.
With cookies made, humor served hot,
Here's to the joy that warms the spot!

Laughter in the Twinkling Glow

In the glow of lights, we sing and dance,
Jingle bells ringing, it's our chance.
With eggnog spills and cookies in hand,
We laugh at the chaos, it's unplanned.

Cats in the tree, oh what a sight,
Tinsel stuck to them, a furry fright.
Gifts wrapped in socks, it's quite the mess,
But our goofy moments, we proudly confess.

Memories in a Sugar Cookie

Baking with flour, a snowy haze,
Frosting on noses, it's a sugar craze.
Gingerbread men that look quite absurd,
With half a smile and a silly word.

Sprinkles flying like a colorful storm,
Cookie disasters that somehow warm.
Burnt edges laugh, we'll use them for crumbs,
In our sweet chaos, the joy still comes.

Wreaths of Joy Unfurled

Wreaths made of laughter and glittery cheer,
Hanging on doors for all to steer.
Neighbors peeking, wonderstruck eyes,
As we sing loudly, with frosty goodbyes.

Bows that are lopsided, what a delight,
Who knew that crafting could lead to a fight?
With hot glue blunders, our fingers are stuck,
Yet through all the mess, we still say, "Good luck!"

A Promise of Peace in the Chill

Winter's cold bite can't chill our fun,
Snowmen with hats and a bright paper gun.
Snowball battles in a fluffy white dome,
In the spirit of joy, we feel right at home.

With cocoa that spills and marshmallows fly,
We build snow forts that reach for the sky.
Laughter erupts as we tumble and roll,
In our snowy wonder, we warm every soul.

Wrapped in Love's Embrace

Tangled lights on the tree, oh what a sight,
A cat in the garland, what a funny fright!
Cookies left half-eaten, crumbs on the floor,
A chocolate thief lurking, can we blame it more?

Grandpa in a sweater, a bit too tight,
Dancing with the turkey, what a comical plight!
Laughter fills the air, like snowflakes that twirl,
In this house of joy, let every heart swirl.

Frosted Windows and Warm Hearts

Frosted windows hide antics inside,
Snowmen look guilty, who had that ride?
Hot cocoa spills, a marshmallow fight,
Winter's quirks make our spirits ignite!

Sledding gone wrong, an epic face plant,
With laughter and giggles, all winter enchant!
Scarves like boa constrictors, too long to wear,
Yet warmth from our smiles fills the brisk air.

A Tapestry of Yuletide Dreams

Stockings are hung with a questionable flair,
Each year we wonder, what's that smell in there?
The children all giggle, as pets launch a spree,
Unwrapping presents, oh wait, what's that, me?

Red-nosed reindeer peeking from every nook,
Caught munching on cookies, with that guilty look!
Wrapping paper fights like confetti in June,
In this jolly mess, we all sing a tune.

The Spirit of Generosity

Gifts that keep growing, a mountain of cheer,
Yet my gift to the dog is all he holds dear!
Uncle Bob with a fruitcake, a mystery still,
Handing it out, we're just hoping it spills.

A secret Santa game turns into a plot,
Tricks and surprises — we've got quite a lot!
With hearts wide open, and joy on display,
Let's share some giggles this holiday way.

Tinsel Dreams and Sugarplum Wishes

Tinsel's stuck in my hair, a true fashion plight,
Sugarplums dance in my dreams every night.
Elves are weighing the gifts with a scale made of cheese,
Santa's diet? Cookies, oh how he does tease!

Candy canes hang from the ceiling with flair,
My cat found a present, now burrowed in there.
Giggles erupt when we all start to sing,
The dog lifts a paw, giving Santa a ring!

Gathered Beneath the Evergreen

Gathered beneath the spruce with lights so bright,
Grandma's made fudge, oh what a sight!
Uncle Joe's snoring, a real festive sound,
While little Timmy's found where the gifts are bound.

Frosty's lost his hat in the age-old game,
He's rolling in snow, but he's got no shame.
The ornaments twinkle, saying, 'Look at us!'
While the puppy runs wild, causing quite the fuss!

Frost-Kissed Memories

Frost-kissed noses and cheeks of bright hue,
Mom's secret cookie recipe, we'll share with the crew!
Dad's dressed as Santa, but lost his fake beard,
Laughter erupts, no one seems to be scared.

Sledding on hills, all bundled up tight,
The snowball fight starts, oh what a sight!
Hot cocoa spills, on my brand-new sweater,
Yet we laugh and we shout, nothing could be better!

A Time for Giving

A time for gifts, but also for pranks,
Dad wraps his own shoes, then thanks all his thanks.
The kids are all giggling, with mischief in eyes,
Keeping their secrets, oh what a surprise!

Laughter fills homes with each silly joke,
While cocoa's been mistaken for some awful smoke.
Gathering laughter, like snowflakes so bright,
We celebrate love, what a warm, cozy night!

In the Company of Loved Ones

Baking cookies, dough in hair,
Laughter echoes everywhere.
Uncle Fred's socks, a sight to see,
Jingle bells, oh what glee!

Wrapping gifts with tape so tight,
Chasing cats, what a fright!
Auntie's hat, it's full of flair,
Poinsettias here, everywhere!

Celestial Snowflakes

Snowflakes dancing from the sky,
Down they swirl, oh my, oh my!
Kids in mittens make a mound,
Snowball fights, loud laughter's found.

Hot cocoa spills, marshmallows fly,
Mama's sweater, two sizes high.
Frosty winks with a carrot nose,
As we march through winter's prose.

Whimsical White Wonders

Twinkling lights on every tree,
Grandpa's snoring, oh, can't we see?
Naps on laps beneath the glow,
While carols tech-rap steal the show!

Silly hats and ugly sweaters,
Pulling pranks, oh, we're trendsetters.
Aerial ornaments, a new sport,
Every mishap we'll retell, of course!

Festive Gatherings and Cheer

Cousins quarrel over the pie,
Sister's trying not to cry.
Champagne popping, cheers abound,
Confetti carpets all around!

Grandma's dance, it's pure delight,
Watch out, she's taken flight!
laughter bubbles, spills and stains,
As joy and chaos intertwains!

Embracing the Night's Magic

Twinkling lights all around,
A squirrel dressed as Santa's found.
With cookies stacked up high in piles,
We giggle at our holiday styles.

The tree's so bright, it's almost blinding,
But look! Is that Uncle Bob, grinding?
He spilled the punch, oh what a sight,
This party's bound to last all night.

Reindeer games on the TV glow,
As cats chase ribbons, stealing the show.
Grandma's knitting with one eye closed,
While Grandpa's snoring, oh how he dozed!

Where's my gift? My list was long,
I swear I asked for a ukulele song.
Instead, I got a fruitcake beast,
I guess I'll have it at the feast!

Where Hearts Find Home

Gather 'round the table, no one's late,
   But Cousin Joe's lost in the bait.
He thought he'd cook, what a surprise,
  We'll feast on cereal, oh how time flies!

The dog dressed like a reindeer paws,
   Chasing after Santa's fake claws.
Kids make snowmen, wonky and round,
But it's the laughter that's the best sound.

The carols echo, but not in tune,
   As Auntie dances with a broom.
The warmth of home, messy yet bright,
 We're merry and silly, oh what a sight!

With lights that flicker like stars above,
    We celebrate this crazy love.
  In every giggle, there's a spark,
  This joyful chaos leaves its mark.

A Tangle of Lights and Hearts

The lights are tangled, a colorful mess,
Dad's wrestling the tree, oh, what duress!
With ornaments misplaced and garlands awry,
Mom says, "It's perfect!" but we just sigh.

As cookies burn in the oven's heat,
The smell of pine can't be beat.
We raid the kitchen, snacks galore,
Good luck keeping us away from the store!

The gingerbread house looks quite surreal,
Though it's leaning like it lost its zeal.
But who cares if it doesn't stand right?
It's still tasty, a sugary delight!

So here's to the laughter, the fond embrace,
Of family fun in this wild race.
With love and joy, we'll sing out loud,
In our tangled mess, we're more than proud.

Under the Winter's Embrace

Snowflakes fall, a fluffy white show,
As laughter erupts, the kids all glow.
The snowman's chubby, his hat askew,
He's got a carrot, yet wants a shoe!

Our sledding adventures lead to a crash,
Let's hope Aunt Maud doesn't completely lash!
Hot cocoa's spilling, marshmallows fly,
As we warm our toes while the fire is nigh.

The pet cat stealing the holiday feast,
With a wink, she thinks she's our best beast.
And oh, that fruitcake—it's still sticking around,
A mystery snack that we just found!

In cozy corners with friends and kin,
We share our stories, let the fun begin.
It's messy and wild, but with glee we sing,
In this frosty world, laughter's the king!

The Warmth of Holiday Lanterns

Lanterns flicker with glee,
Casting shadows wild and free.
Santa's got a belly laugh,
Trying to fit into a sleigh half.

Snowmen dance with carrot nose,
In a tango, striking a pose.
Frosty gives a wink and grin,
But trips and lands in a trash bin!

Cats in bows, the dogs in hats,
Chasing lights, oh how they prance!
Footprints lead to cookies gone,
Rats are tipped off; they munch till dawn.

Friends appear with joy in hand,
With gifts that no one can understand.
A sweater knitted for a cat?
The world needs laughter—that's a fact!

Joy in Every Ornament

Ornament on the tree, it swings,
Let's hang a pickle, see what it brings.
Uncle Joe lost his mind last year,
Saying that the gnome is full of cheer!

Tinsel tangled in the cat's fur,
As he stalks the garland—a fuzzy blur.
Grandma claims it's a family heirloom,
But it's just a dusty old broom!

Treats are hidden all around,
That chocolate stash? Now it's never found!
A cat burglar has crept this night,
Leaving paw prints, what a sight!

With bells that jingle, and folks that sing,
It's time to laugh and let joy spring.
So unearth the lights, let mischief out,
'Tis the season for giggles, no doubt!

Echoes of Caroling Hearts

Carolers jingle in a row,
But the dog thinks it's a show!
Barking out a tune so sweet,
With every woof, he takes the lead.

Muffin tops and giggles spread,
As they scuttle, almost dead.
Did he just hit a high note?
Or was it breakfast he forgot to tote?

Couples twirl, beneath the moon,
Tripping over each other's shoes.
Laughter rings through frosty air,
As someone loses their sweater pair!

If laughter's music, we're in tune,
With hiccuping choir—what a boon!
So carol, but don't drop the beat,
'Cause falling snow is soft, but not that sweet!

Laughter Beneath the Mistletoe

Gather 'round, there's kisses to steal,
But Uncle Bob's made it a meal!
He missed the mistletoe cue,
And kissed the pot roast instead of you.

Under the greens where giggles thrive,
Watch out for Grandma, she's still alive!
With a wink and a cheeky little grin,
She'll swipe your cookie and dance with kin!

What's this? A parrot in bow tie?
Squawking "Merry!" as you pass by.
Bright red cheeks and playful cheer,
Beneath the leaves, laughter we hear.

As the clock strikes midnight with squawks,
It's time to dance in mismatched socks!
Raise a glass, and toast to the night,
Wit and joy make everything right!

Blessings Beneath the Tree

Beneath the tree, gifts do await,
A cat with flair, claims the best fate.
Tinsel in her claws, what a sight!
As bows go flying, oh what a fright!

Grandpa's snoring, a festive tune,
While Auntie dances, a lopsided swoon.
Cookies vanishing, where do they go?
Must've been Santa, or a cheeky snow!

The twinkling lights, all tangled and tight,
A yearly battle, who'll win the fight?
Yet laughter erupts, we try to untwine,
It's chaos, but really, it's simply divine!

So here's to the quirks, the joy we receive,
In moments like these, it's love we believe.
With giggles and grumbles, the best we agree,
Are blessings that sprout from under the tree.

Unity in the Frosty Air

Frosty air calls for laughter bright,
Snowmen we build, but none stand right.
One falls in giggles, another's a mess,
While a dog snatches, what a snowy guess!

Sledding down hills, screaming with glee,
The neighbor's cat thinks it's all just a spree.
Snowballs are flying, but watch out for me,
I'm dodging and ducking, like a duck from a bee!

Bundled so tight, can hardly move,
The mittens are gone, who did that groove?
Hot cocoa spills, and marshmallows fly,
Sipping too fast, oh my, oh my!

As the night falls, we gather to cheer,
Sharing our tales, with laughter sincere.
So raise up your mug, let silly times grow,
In the frosty air, our joy's on show!

Footprints on the Snowy Path

Footprints in snow lead a merry way,
But surely those were made by a stray?
Chasing that squirrel, oh what a thrill,
Turns out it's just me, slipping down hill!

Treading so lightly, I whisper a song,
When suddenly, a shoe's gone wrong!
My toe's on the edge, but who needs a shoe?
When dancing in snow brings the fun I pursue!

Each footprint a story, each slip a delight,
My scarf caught a branch, but I'm holding on tight.
With giggles surrounding, the world is aglow,
In this playful dance, we let our hearts flow!

And as night descends on our snowy spree,
We warm by the fire, with cookies and tea.
So here's to the frolics, the slips and the laughs,
On this curious journey, we make our own paths.

A Serenade of Hope

A jingle of bells echoes with laughter,
Standing in line for hot cocoa, oh what a disaster!
Sprinkles on tops, but they're too much to bear,
One sip too fast, and cocoa's everywhere!

Grandma's old stories come out with glee,
Of big hairy Santa, trapped in the tree.
We hang our stockings, but where do they land?
I claim the pink one, with glitter so grand!

The cookies are gone, did the elves sneak a bite?
With crumbs on their faces, what a silly sight!
Each giggly moment turns our fate bright,
With mishaps and laughter, we feel just right!

So raise up your voice, a joyful accord,
In this time of wonder, let laughter be stored.
For hope is a song, that dances along,
In the hearts of the merry, where we all belong!

Secrets of the Hearth

Underneath the snowy skies,
The cookies hide in clever guise.
Elves in the pantry, what a sight!
They snack all day and dance all night.

In the oven, pies do sing,
'Til Grandma claims them, "It's my thing!"
With sprinkles bright and frosting wild,
The cat leaps in, he thinks he's styled.

The tree is up, or so they say,
But lights are tangled in disarray.
As tangled as my Christmas cheer,
I think the gifts are hiding here!

With laughter ringing through the halls,
Our spirit flies, despite the falls.
So grab a cookie or a treat,
Join in the fun, it can't be beat!

A Journey to the Heart of Home

In grandma's house, the fun begins,
With mismatched socks, we wear our sins.
Heated debates on who can't cook,
While burning bread takes center look.

The reindeer games are such a mess,
Who knew they'd end up in distress?
Tinsel flies and toys go zoom,
As Uncle Bob grows bored in gloom.

The kids all scream for snowball fights,
While Dad just aims at festive lights.
The snowmen look quite plump and round,
You'd think they fell instead of found!

So gather round, let laughter rise,
With cheeks all red and twinkling eyes.
For every moment, joy does roam,
It truly makes a jolly home!

Candlelit Wishes

With flick'ring flames and shadows play,
The cake's too big for us today!
Let's light a wish and watch it soar,
Even if it lands on the floor.

The stockings hang with hope and cheer,
But someone's borrowed them, I fear.
A puppy's dream caught in a snare,
Inside the stocking, totally bare.

Laughter echoes through the night,
While Dad's stuck in the Christmas light.
Mom's out searching for the wine,
And the gingerbread? It's quite divine!

So raise a glass, let jests prevail,
In every mishap, love's the trail.
Amidst the fun, let's take a bow,
For candlelit wishes guide us now!

The Magic of Shared Moments

The mistletoe hangs, my fate is sealed,
A kiss from Aunt Marie, who's grilled!
My cheeks are red; I dodge and duck,
This Christmas cheer is quite the luck!

The games commence with fits of giggles,
While Auntie's cat performs its wiggles.
The fruitcake bounces, will it survive?
At least it helps the dog to thrive!

A puzzle's missing pieces abound,
Get ready for chaos, joy's all around.
The neighbors freeze as we sing loud,
In such delight, we feel so proud.

So gather close, hold on tight,
In every laugh, we find the light.
For every moment shared so dear,
Creates the spirit year by year!

The Essence of Holiday Cheer

In the kitchen pies are made,
A cat is there, a sly charade.
The tree's adorned with tinsel bright,
A squirrel just stole the star last night.

Stockings hung but filled with socks,
By Uncle Joe who loves his knocks.
A gingerbread man starts to dance,
And suddenly gets lost in a trance.

The plates are full, but so's the floor,
A dog comes in, he wants some more.
With laughter ringing through the hall,
We trip on toys, but have a ball.

The essence here, it's plain to see,
Is all this joy and funny glee.
With family quirks and love to share,
In this wild whirl, we have a flair.

Embracing Hope's Gentle Glow

In a world where snowmen sing,
And carolers wear a cheeky ring.
The lights outshine the stars above,
As penguins skate, they laugh, they shove.

Hope's gentle glow, a twinkling light,
That makes the grumpy neighbor bright.
With cookies baked that crumble fast,
A foodie's dream, but not built to last.

The candles flicker—oops, not one!
As grandma thinks it's time for fun.
Her stories spin like holiday yarn,
About a time when everything's a charm.

In the end, we share a smile,
As silly jokes go on for a while.
With joy wrapped up like gifts we throw,
The warmth ignites the hearts we know.

Mirth and Music in the Air

Mirth and music in every room,
With whistling tunes and a whiff of plume.
The reindeer prance in holiday hats,
While grandpa sings 'bout charming cats.

The cookies vanish at the speed of light,
The kids speed up in a dance delight.
With mistletoe hung at every turn,
A sister squeals—'My crush will never learn!'

Outdoors the snowflakes bring a dance,
But not for long, it's too much chance.
With snowball fights and sleds in tow,
It's a race to see who'll take the show.

In this scene of laughter's sway,
We'll treasure each and every play.
As music plays and spirits soar,
Mirth connects us, forevermore.

A Melody of Kindred Spirits

A melody of laughs and cheers,
With every note, it staves off fears.
A trio sings, one off the beat,
While cat jumps up to take the seat.

Sweet candy canes and coffee spills,
Mix with laughter, space for thrills.
The family car trip's filled with clatter,
As songs blast loud, who minds the chatter?

With jokes and puns that spin about,
The awkwardness we try to route.
The toast is made, a sip, a cheer,
In this warm glow, we hold so dear.

Together we find joy at play,
In quirky ways that guide the day.
With every smile and hearty huddle,
A song of love in all the muddle.

Stars and Stockings Alight

The stockings hang, all stuffed with care,
Filled with goodies, a sweet affair.
But in the night, a sneaky cat,
Tore through gifts, imagine that!

With twinkling stars that laugh and play,
They wink at us, then dance away.
A cookie left for Santa's fun,
Replaced by crumbs, oh what a run!

The tree's adorned with tinsel bright,
While lights flicker, oh what a sight!
Yet here comes Fido, in full delight,
Knocked it down, oh what a fright!

So here's to all the festive cheer,
With giggles ringing far and near.
Forget perfection, let chaos reign,
'Ts a merry time, with laughs and gain!

Echoes of the Evergreen

In the corner lurks a tree so grand,
With needles sharp, like a prickly band.
Ornaments sparkle with stories bold,
But the cat thinks it's a jungle, behold!

The scent of pine fills the air with glee,
As Uncle Joe spills cider with a spree.
A toast to cheer, he raises his cup,
O'er his own feet, he trips and flops up!

Children play with snowballs tight,
While Aunt Sally's outfit gives quite a fright.
With sequins that twinkle and jingle bells,
Her fashion sense is a story that sells!

So gather 'round, with laughter to share,
In this festive havoc, there's love everywhere.
Forget the norm, let's raise a cheer,
For joyful chaos, let's all draw near!

Tales of Frost and Friendship

On frosty nights with laughter bright,
We gather 'round, under moonlight.
Snowmen towering, look so proud,
While snowflakes chuckle, laughing loud!

Hot cocoa spills on a fuzzy sock,
As we engage in a pillow rock.
The marshmallows dance on top in delight,
While tales of friendship warm the night!

Gifts exchanged with a wink and a grin,
"Did I get you socks, or did you win?"
Amidst the giggles, a playful chase,
Laughter erupts, filling the space.

So here's to joy in this frosty glow,
With bonds of warmth that only grow.
Forget the fuss, just hold on tight,
To tales of love that dance in the light!

Lanterns in the Softest Night

When evening falls, the lanterns glow,
Presents wrapped all in a row.
But hiding 'neath that shiny wrap,
Is a toy that goes 'whirr' and 'zap'.

Grandma's cookies, oh what a seduction,
Yet there's a slight cookie destruction.
With crumbs scattered, here and there,
The dog thinks he's the new millionaire!

In the stillness, laughter floats,
While kids exchange their winter coats.
The mittens clash, the hats go askew,
What's Christmas without a silly view?

So raise a cheer, let the laughter ring,
For all the joy that this season brings.
With hearts aglow, in the darkest night,
We're all just stars, sharing our light!

Stars Above a Silent Night

The stars are winking, oh what a sight,
A reindeer's lost GPS, it's took a flight.
Santa's stuck in the chimney, what a fuss,
His belly's too big, but we don't discuss.

The snowman's hat is two sizes too big,
He dances like a pro, doing a jig.
Elves are outnumbered, by cookies galore,
They're all sugared up, can't take anymore.

Frosty's gone wild with a snowball fight,
Launching frosty lumps under the moonlight.
His carrot nose wiggles, with every throw,
Making sure that he steals the whole show.

The night's full of laughter, the fun never ends,
With jingling bells, and all of our friends.
Hot cocoa spills while we sing a tune,
Laughter echoes, bright as the moon.

Snowflakes Dancing Down

Snowflakes falling with giggles and cheer,
They tickle your nose, as they draw near.
Everyone's bundled, all snug and tight,
But one scarf is missing, it's put up a fight.

A snowball sneezes, then flies through the air,
Lands on a penguin who didn't care.
He flaps and he flies, acting all cool,
While kids slide down hills, breaking every rule.

The snowmen debate on who wears it best,
A top hat or bucket, put them to the test.
They gossip and giggle, it's all in good fun,
Under the sparkle, we play till we're done.

As the evening settles, the stars twist and twirl,
The laughter and joy make our heads all swirl.
With cocoa on lips and snowflakes in hair,
We dance with delight, without a single care.

Feasts and Festivities

The kitchen's a circus, flour in the air,
Grandma's got cookies with sprinkles to share.
Someone burns toast, a soft scream escapes,
The turkey's on strike, no matter how it shapes.

The table's a mess, with plates piled high,
Someone's lost a fork, oh me, oh my!
Cranberry sauce that looks like a blob,
Yet everyone claims it's the best for the job.

A battle of pies erupts in the night,
Pumpkin vs. apple, it's quite the sight.
Whipped cream's on noses, and laughter turns loud,
As we toast to our chaos, all family proud.

With stories of old, we gather around,
For feasts full of laughter, together we're bound.
Our hearts full of joy — and belts that are tight,
As we roll homeward, blissfully bright.

The Magic of Flickering Flames

Through the crackling fire, we share our tales,
Of socks overflowing with silly males.
A log rolls too close, sends the sparkles high,
We all jump like fish, as the embers fly.

The stockings are stuffed, but look for the cat,
He's claimed them all — think he's quite the brat.
"Who ate the last cookie?" we ponder in jest,
The crumbs on his whiskers give quite the quest.

A game of charades is about to unfold,
With dad in a costume that looks quite bold.
Laughter erupts with each silly act,
As the warmth of the fire keeps the giggles intact.

As the night wears on, we bask in the glow,
The flickering dance puts on quite the show.
With love all around, and jokes that won't cease,
We celebrate magic… with laughter and peace.

Harmony in Christmas Colors

Red noses and green hats, oh what a sight,
The snowman on the lawn is ready for a fight.
Decorations tangled, but we're filled with cheer,
Santa's reindeer laugh at our holiday sneer.

Elves in pajamas, sipping hot cocoa flows,
While Grandma wraps gifts, tightly with bows.
The lights on the roof flicker like stars,
Just don't ask to borrow the big red car!

Laughter's our gift, wrapped up with delight,
In this colorful chaos, everything's bright.
Snowballs are flying, kids run and scream,
While Dad dons a sweater that's fit for a meme.

Together we sing, songs all out of tune,
Cheering as we dance, maybe under the moon.
A holiday jingle, with laughter it swells,
In harmony we blend, like those jingle bells!

The Taste of Togetherness

Cookies all scattered, flour in the air,
Mom's secret recipe, we all want to share.
Burnt ones in the oven, a crispy delight,
"Don't eat those!" she shouts, "You'll be up all night!"

We slice up the ham, oh what a grand feast,
A turkey that sings, "Please don't call me beast!"
Potatoes so mashed, they're creamy and swirled,
Just don't ask for seconds, our diet's unfurled.

Desserts piled high, the table's a dream,
Chocolate and caramel, an avalanche stream.
"No more room!" we cry, then moan and we sigh,
As Aunt Edna pulls out her famous fruit pie!

Gathered around, each bite met with glee,
As stories are shared, and laughter runs free.
The taste of this season, a feast from above,
It's all about sharing, and feeling the love!

Touches of Love and Kindness

A pinch of compassion, a sprinkle of cheer,
We hug like we mean it, my goodness, my dear!
With mittens and scarves, we bundle up tight,
While carolers harmonize into the night.

The notes of a piano, ring out with such flair,
While the cat knocks the tree down, that rascal beware!
Gifts wrapped in laughter, with ribbons and bows,
Grandpa's socks are the hottest new clothes!

The laughter of children, a sweet symphony,
Building a snowman, just you and me.
With twinkling lights strung on every small tree,
Our hearts filled with joy, like we're all meant to be.

A wink and a smile, the warmth fills the air,
In a world made of kindness, we nourish our care.
The little moments matter, in this season so bright,
With touches of love, we keep spirits light!

The Cheer of Chilly Evenings

Chilly evenings come with a cozy embrace,
Hot cocoa in hand, we slow down the pace.
With blankets all piled, and popcorn on hand,
The best family movie, oh isn't it grand?

Our snowmen wear hats, and they sip on tea,
While snowflakes are dancing, stars from a spree.
A snowball fight brewing, outside on the lawn,
But first, let's finish this episode, come on!

Silly jokes swapped, as we gather so tight,
With shadows and giggles, we stretch into night.
Grandma's old stories infect us with glee,
As poppers explode, like a wild jubilee!

So let's raise a cheer for these evenings so sweet,
With laughter and warmth, we gather to meet.
In chilly December, with hearts all aglow,
We celebrate moments, we laugh, we bestow!

Creating Memories in the Frost

Snowflakes dance like giggling sprites,
As we build a snowman, with coal for sights.
Carrot nose, a scarf, and a hat so fine,
We laugh till we drop, sipping hot cocoa divine.

Sledding down hills with shouts and glee,
It's a race to the bottom; come join me!
With snow in our pants and big frosty grins,
We tumble and roll until the fun begins.

The dog steals the mittens and runs in the snow,
We chase him in circles; oh, what a show!
Captured by laughter and moments so bright,
Creating memories in the frosty night.

As the stars twinkle high, the chill fills the air,
We head inside where it's cozy and fair.
With cookies in hand and stories to share,
The season's delight is beyond all compare.

The Story of Giving

A gift wrapped in laughter, with a side of cheer,
Beneath the tree, oh, the magic is here!
A sock stuffed with folly, a tie that's too loud,
We giggle and gasp, all part of the crowd.

Uncle Joe re-gifting his last year's surprise,
With a wink and a nod, he winks with his eyes.
A sweater that's knitted with love and some care,
"Who wore it better?" we tease and we stare.

A fruitcake that bounces like a rubbery ball,
"Who will take this home?" we all have a call.
The story of giving, so quirky, so sweet,
With laughter and love, our hearts skip a beat.

Wrapped in the echoes of holiday cheer,
With friends all around, we spread joy far and near.
In the spirit of fun, let the laughter not cease,
The gift of each moment brings us great peace.

A Time to Share, A Time to Care

When the bell rings loud and carolers sing,
We gather together, it's a magical thing.
Hot cider abounds, and the cookies are baked,
Oh, the stories we tell and the laughs that we make.

With cousins and uncles and family galore,
We play games of charades till our sides are sore.
A clever charade with missteps so grand,
We laugh till we cry, unplanned and unplanned.

As we swap tales of the year that has flown,
They get funnier still just as ice cream is thrown.
A time to share joy, a time to declare,
In the silliness found, there's so much we care.

So let's lift our cups high to the moments we share,
With warmth in our hearts and laughter in the air.
For the spirit that glows when family appears,
Is what holds us together through all of our years.

Reflections of a Joyful Past

The lights twinkle bright, just like in a dream,
We dance with the memories, oh how they gleam.
Grandma's old recipes, the fails and the wins,
We can't stop the laughter as the chaos begins.

Remember that one year, the turkey was burned?
With smoke in the air, oh how we all turned!
We feasted on leftovers, with a side of despair,
Yet somehow, we laughed, and we didn't care.

The moments we treasure, like ornaments hung,
Crafted with mischief in each ball that's flung.
In our hearts we carry a playful hearted blast,
Reflections of joy from a time long passed.

So gather around, let the memories spin,
With joyful reminders tucked deep within.
For laughter and love are the gifts we must keep,
As we cherish the past and the secrets we reap.

The Light within the Darkness

In December nights, the lights all twinkle,
I tripped on a cord, my foot got a wrinkle.
The cat in the tree gave a sideways glance,
Even he knows it's a holiday dance.

Cookies are baked, but I might have missed,
A key ingredient, oh what a twist!
The cookies are crunchy, like rocks they relate,
'Twas a lesson in baking, but I'm feeling great.

Kids with their lists, they're ready to shout,
Praying for toys, or a drum that won't clout.
Mom's sipping cocoa, she just moved the tree,
Watch out for ornaments, they fall like confetti!

Sledding down hills, in a wild rush we go,
Snowballs like cannonballs, watch out below!
The laughter is loud, through the cold winter air,
Who knew winter fun would come with such flair?

Kindness Wrapped in Ribbons

With ribbons ablaze, I'm a gift wrappin' pro,
Last year's mishap, well now I know.
Scissors in hand, I feel like a champ,
But the cat thinks my treasures are all just a camp!

Uncle Joe's treat? A fruitcake supreme,
Slice it up nice, it's more like a dream.
The neighbors all giggle when they stop by to greet,
"Have you tried our Aunt Maude's top-secret sweet?"

Grandma's got stories, of Christmas long past,
Each tale gets weirder, but we're having a blast.
"Remember the time the lights caught on fire?"
We laugh till we snort, each moment we desire.

So here's to the laughter, the glee, and the fun,
Wrapped with good humor, our work's never done.
Here's to sweet kindness, in packages bright,
Bringing warmth to the chilly, enchanting night!

Fireside Reflections

Gathered by fire, we toast marshmallows wide,
But half of them end up charred, we try to hide.
With cocoa in hand, and spirits to lift,
Dad tells the tale of his most favorite gift.

The dog trots in, with a sock as his prize,
Who knew he'd find joy in a treasure that flies?
With laughter and twinklers, our hearts feel so light,
Misadventures galore make the flames dance just right.

Hot chocolate spills, oh what a sight to behold,
A chocolate mustache, to the children so bold.
A dance of reflections in the glow of the fire,
Full of giggles and tales, they never tire.

As the night wraps us snug, by the flickering flame,
We cherish these moments that can't be the same.
Each chuckle and whisper, shared close by the heat,
Fashion memories sweeter than any treat!

The Dance of Giving

In a flurry of snow, gifts spinning around,
Wrappings are flying, chaos abound.
A scarf for my dad, two sizes too small,
He'll wear it with pride, or not wear it at all!

The kids are all bouncing, with energy grand,
For cookies and candy, they finally planned.
Gingerbread houses look more like mush,
But who needs perfection? Just give it a rush!

With hats on our heads and mittens that clash,
We dance through the street, bringing joy in a splash.
With laughter and gleam, the spirit runs wild,
All ages together, just each one a child.

So here's to the moments, the laughter we share,
Wrapped up and tied with a soft, loving care.
In this dance of giving, we meld through the night,
Creating our joy, like stars shining bright!

The Heartstrings of the Holidays

In December's chill, we deck the halls,
With sparkly lights and inflatable balls.
Grandma's fruitcake? A real test of might,
We toss it around like a snowball fight.

The carolers sing, all off-key and loud,
Jingle bells ringing, attracting a crowd.
But Uncle Joe's dancing, oh what a sight,
He spins on his toes, and then ends up in fright.

Eggnog spills over, it's quite the delight,
The pets taste the cookies, then vanish from sight.
The tree is a leaner, a bit of a flop,
But we gather 'round, and we just can't stop.

So raise up a glass, let's toast with a grin,
To laughter and chaos, let the fun begin!
In this wondrous season, let's dance, laugh and cheer,
With memories made, it's the best time of year!

Voices of Celebration

With mistletoe strung up, we stand and we sway,
A dance party's formed, come join the ballet.
A cat in a Santa hat perches on high,
While dodging the chaos, it gives us a sigh.

The cookies are burnt, but who really cares?
We've got eggnog in mugs and love in the airs.
The neighbor's loud music is blaring all night,
But it's all part of fun; we're feeling all right.

Kids bouncing off walls, like rockets in flight,
The holidays sparkle, but not quite so bright.
A game of charades that's way out of tune,
The punch bowl erupts, like a festive balloon.

So gather around, let the silliness show,
With tales that we tell, and laughter that flows.
These moments we cherish, they come with some quirks,
In this fight for the future, we all are the jerks!

Whispers of Frosty Nights

Frost bites our noses, we zip up so tight,
A snowman's got style, dressed up just right.
His eyes are made from coal, and carrots for noses,
But kids pick his arms, are we playing with poses?

The sleigh bells ring as we dash through the snow,
But wait! Is that Santa? A reindeer in tow?
He's stuck in the chimney, we giggle and tease,
Will he fit with all those cookies and cheese?

Wrapping presents, what a challenging feat,
With tape that gets tangled around our own feet.
We laugh as we struggle with scissors gone wild,
And find out the gifts were for Mom, not the child.

So light up the night with twinkling delight,
With love and some chaos, everything feels right.
We'll treasure the laughter, the warmth and the cheer,
Frosty nights whisper joy when family is near!

Heartstrings Twinkling

The lights on the tree flicker, oh what a show,
A family of ornaments put on a woe.
Grandma's cat's climbing, all limbs in a tangle,
As he swipes at the baubles, the decorations dangle.

Christmas sweaters worn, the colors collide,
With patterns so wild, you can't help but hide.
The pets are all restless, a holiday mess,
Caught stealing the gifts, we can't help but press.

We gather in warmth, sipping cocoa so rich,
But someone drops marshmallows, oh, what a glitch!
With laughter like music, our hearts all entwined,
We cherish these moments with love so aligned.

So here's to the laughter, the chaos sublime,
With hearts that are twinkling, what joy in our rhyme.
In this season of cheer, we find what we seek,
The smiles we have now, the memories we keep!

Echoes of Laughter in the Snow

Snowflakes fall, oh what a sight,
Snowmen dance in the moonlight.
Kids in boots, with cheeks all red,
Tossing snow, forget their bed.

Hot cocoa spills, it's quite the mess,
Sipping slowly, no need to stress.
Marshmallows float, like tiny dreams,
Laughter echoes, bursting at the seams.

Sledding down hills, oh what a glide,
Squeals of joy, no one can hide.
A snowball fight, epic and grand,
Victory dances in the white land.

So come along, join in the play,
Make these moments, here to stay.
With giggles and fun, we'll explore,
Crafting memories forevermore.

Cradles of Comfort and Joy

Underneath the twinkling lights,
Gifts wrapped tight, oh what delights!
Grandma's cookies, a secret stash,
Funny cat wrestles the wrapping trash.

Singing carols, off-key and loud,
Join the fun, be merry and proud.
Uncle Joe's jokes, makes us all groan,
What's the deal with this fruitcake alone?

A cozy fire, hot nog in hand,
Awkward dance moves, we all understand.
A quirky sweater, bright and bold,
Making fun of the fashion of old.

With laughter ringing through the night,
We celebrate joy, oh so bright.
Hugging each other, our hearts align,
In this crazy warmth, we intertwine.

The Silent Night's Promise

The night is quiet, but not for long,
As giggles bubble, we join the throng.
Whispers of secrets, the twinkling trees,
A mischievous cat swipes at the leaves.

Santa's sleigh might be late this year,
While we all snack on the festive cheer.
Elves on strike, where could they be?
Hiding away with our last candy!

Frosty nose peeking through the frost,
Searching for something, what's truly lost?
A jingle bell here, a cookie crumb there,
Join in the fun, if you dare!

The promise of joy wrapped in delight,
In the silliness, we find our light.
So gather 'round, let laughter take flight,
In this silent night, it's out of sight!

A Pathway of Light and Love

As we wander through glimmering lanes,
Lighted paths, joy remains.
A parade of folks, all dressed so bright,
Riding their bikes, what a funny sight!

Murals of laughter grace every wall,
Cats in scarves join the snowy brawl.
Wobbling reindeer, clumsy and fun,
Chasing each other, just on the run.

Cookies shaped like all sorts of glee,
Gingerbread houses, wonky as can be.
Frosted windows, laughter galore,
Snowflakes pirouetting, never a bore.

In this curious season, love fills the air,
With joy and mischief, there's none to spare.
Every corner and turn, giggles appear,
On this bright path, we hold dear!

Joy in Every Heartbeat

In the kitchen, cookies bake,
Elves in aprons make mistakes.
Frosting fights and giggles loud,
Sugar highs—oh, we're so proud!

Trees adorned with wacky flair,
Lights that twinkle, spark, and scare.
Unruly pets in tinsel bound,
Decorations all around!

Socks that vanish, time to fret,
Did the dog eat them? You bet!
Wrapped-up gifts in silly shapes,
Scissors, ribbons, endless tapes!

Cheers erupt in snowy cheer,
Frosty friends we hold so dear.
Laughter fills the chilly night,
Jolly gathers, pure delight!

Whispers of Yuletide Cheer

Snowmen wobble, hats askew,
Carrots fly; oh, what a view!
Gingerbread men on the run,
'Tis the season—let's have fun!

Mismatched socks on every chair,
Pine-scented chaos fills the air.
Silly songs on repeat play,
Dancing like it's holiday!

Secret Santa's crafty schemes,
Unwrapping leads to shocked screams.
Who thought socks were such a win?
Next year, no one will begin!

Joyful spirits in the air,
Mittens lost beyond repair.
Hot cocoa spills, it's quite a sight,
Laughter truly steals the night!

A Tapestry of Winter Light

Lights all tangled, what a sight,
Cursing gently, oh so bright!
Wrapped around the old cat's tail,
Let's hope Santa brings no mail!

Mittens worn with holes galore,
Neighbors laugh, then knock the door.
Cookies crumbling, flour flies,
No one's safe from baking pies!

Chasing snowflakes, dogs all bark,
Caroling till way past dark.
Merry chaos fills the street,
Sledding stunts—it's pure retreat!

As we gather, hugs abound,
Spill some punch, dance all around.
In this season, hearts ignite,
Laughter shines, a festive light!

The Warmth of Gathering

Gather 'round, but mind the cakes,
Sisters argue over flakes.
Mashed potatoes, lumpy art,
But it's love that fills the heart!

Cousins bicker, who's the best?
Checkmate moves, we're all obsessed.
Laughter echoes, tales retold,
Holiday spirit—and some gold!

Merry sweaters, knitted wide,
Brothers cringe in fashion pride.
Gloves and hats all mismatched too,
Family quirks shine brightly through!

In the warmth, the chatter flows,
Sweet surprises, candy bows.
This delight, it's hearts we spark,
Growing joy, our funny mark!

Collecting Moments, Not Things

Gifts wrapped tight, much to my plight,
A sock from Uncle Joe, what a sight!
Bows and ribbons, oh what a fuss,
I'll take a laugh, just hand me a bus.

Family chaos, the love we trace,
Tangled lights, a holiday race.
Grandma's cookie dough, now that's a steal,
Mom's fruitcake? I'll just swap for a meal!

Laughter echoes, a joyous cheer,
Pinch a turkey, let's eat, my dear!
The best of seasons, let's toast and sing,
I'd rather memories than any bling.

So here's to mishaps, and funny jokes,
This Christmas spirit, we'll raise our Probes!
Collecting moments, oh what a fling,
I'll take a fall, for joy that we bring.

Brightening Each Others' Days

Socks that don't match, fashion delight,
A tie that's so bright, it's blinding light!
Ho-ho-ho, we laugh all around,
Each silly moment, true joy does abound.

Jingle bells ringing, it's out of tune,
But who needs tunes, when you have a spoon?
We bake and we break, oh what a mess,
But with all this laughter, we feel so blessed!

Mismatched the tree, a crown on a cat,
Rolling in laughter, just look at that!
Each goofy grinning, takes the lead,
In this festive madness, we all succeed.

Let's brighten our days with giggles galore,
And dance all around, till we can't take more!
With love and joy, we'll surely amaze,
The magic is found in these funny days.

The Gift of Presence

The best kind of gift is not what you buy,
But laughing so hard you just want to cry.
A hug from a neighbor, a wink from a friend,
With laughter and love, the fun never ends.

Presents unwrapped, oh what a thrill,
A box of ol' socks? Oh, what a chill!
But hey, who needs fancy, or shiny and bright,
When a belly full of laughter feels just right?

Hot cocoa spilling, marshmallows fly,
Each moment we share, oh me, oh my!
So gather around, let's have a blast,
For joy is the gift that always will last.

So here we are, with mischief and glee,
In this merry chaos, we're truly free.
With giggles to share and stories to tell,
The greatest of presents is keeping us well.

Mirth Among the Snow

Snowflakes are falling, what a bright sight,
We slip and we slide, oh what a fright!
Make a snowman? With a hat that's too big,
He's a real fashionista, just look at him jig!

Caroling loudly, we're off-key but bold,
Our voices like thunder, or so we're told!
Each note causes giggles, and that's just fine,
With holiday cheer, we entwine like a vine.

Giant snowballs flying, a fun little war,
Just watch out for faces, or you might hit the floor!
With red noses glowing, the warmth feels divine,
In this winter wonder, true joy we define.

So raise up your mittens, embrace all the fun,
These silly moments are a true holiday run!
With laughter and snow, our hearts will ignite,
In mirth among the snow, everything feels right.

Bright Eyes in the Candlelight

Little Timmy's eyes shine bright,
Chasing shadows in the night.
Mom's baking cookies, what a smell!
Dropping sprinkles, oh so well!

Dad's got his Christmas sweater on,
Singing loud, though he's all wrong.
The cat's in the tree, oh what a sight,
As ornaments fall, it's pure delight!

Grandma's knitting with her favorite yarn,
Yelling at the kids to not cause harm.
With giggles and laughter, we join in,
Who knew chaos could feel like a win!

In this house of joyful cheer,
The funny moments bring us near.
With bright eyes and hearts aglow,
Each silly moment makes love grow!

Together Under the Same Sky

Bundled up like happy bears,
Snowflakes land on tousled hair.
Hot cocoa spills, what a mess!
But laughter makes it all a success!

Carols sung off-key again,
Neighbors cheer and count to ten.
Who needs harmony in the night?
We're all in this, wrong feels so right!

Sledding down the hill with flair,
Someone yells, watch out for the chair!
We tumble down, and then we see,
Joy's a chorus, wild and free!

Gather 'round the fire, stay warm,
We'll share more tales that bring alarm.
With laughter loud and hearts so spry,
Let's keep on smiling under the same sky!

A Treetop Star Shining

Up on the tree, a star does twinkle,
Dad's on the ladder, oh what a crinkle!
"Just one more bulb!" he proclaims with glee,
The tree shakes, is it falling, or is it me?

Little ones dance round the bright lights,
Till the dog joins in, barking with fright.
Tinsel flies like a glitter bomb,
We pile it on, 'til it looks like a prom!

Mom's trying to calm the holiday craze,
While uncle Fred just loves to amaze.
Cracking jokes with a wink and a grin,
This is the laughter that pulls us in!

So let's raise a toast to the wild ride,
With a treetop star that shines with pride!
Each twinkle tells us we're here to stay,
In our funny, festive, crazy way!

Rhythms of Joy in Every Heart

With a jingle and a bell, the fun begins,
Kids run amok with their cheeky grins.
Wrapping paper covers the floor,
Who needs a box? Let's just adore!

Socks filled with goodies, a true delight,
Finding old toys we thought took flight.
Mom's culinary experiments take the stage,
Dinner's served, though we might need a gauge!

The doorbell rings, it's more guests here,
With hugs and jokes that spread good cheer.
We'll dance and sing till the moon shines bright,
Each laugh that echoes is pure delight!

So here's to joy and laughter's embrace,
In every heart, we find our place.
With rhythms of fun, we cheerfully start,
Creating memories, oh so smart!

Radiant Joy in Winter's Embrace

In the snowy chill, we dance around,
With socks on our feet, sliding on the ground.
Laughter echoes, as we take a fall,
Hot cocoa in hand, we still have a ball.

Neighbors peeking from frosty abodes,
Wishing for cookies, crafting some codes.
We bake and we burn, but who really cares?
Each muffin a trophy, of kitchen affairs.

Snowflakes a-flying, we wear them like hats,
Tangled up mittens, with playful spats.
Snowmen are bickering over their noses,
While inside the warmth, the laughter just glows.

A season of cheer, with whimsical bliss,
Every hug and each laugh, a magical kiss.
In this winter wonder, with spirits so bright,
We find joy in the chaos, in winter's soft light.

Strings of Lights and Smiles

Twinkling lights on the rickety tree,
Tinsel so tangled, it giggles with glee.
We argue and fumble, who hangs it up right?
All in good fun, as we laugh through the night.

Carolers stumble, off-key and loud,
We cheer them along, feeling quite proud.
With hotdogs in hand, it's a festive affair,
As we gather around, laughter fills the air.

Cookies half-eaten, some bathed in sprinkles,
Our faces are messy, just look at our crinkles.
We trade off our sweets, no one knows who's had more,
It's a sugar-filled frenzy, a holiday war.

With each tangled bulb and silly mishap,
We cherish the moments, a heartfelt clap.
So raise up your cup, let's toast to the cheer,
For joy has a way of drawing us near.

The Gift of Togetherness

Gathered around, the family draws close,
With mismatched socks, an earnest hellos.
We swap tales of shame, and giggle some more,
Like Auntie's bad sweater, we just can't ignore.

Granny's at it, with her famous fruitcake,
A rock-hard creation, for goodness' sake!
We keep it a secret, won't tell her the news,
That no one actually eats it, just chew it like blues.

Presents piled up, in a chaotic grin,
With tape stuck to fingers, and paper-like skin.
Under the tree, we uncover good cheer,
Each gift is a memory, wrapped tight with no fear.

So, gather your pals, it's time to unite,
With silly old games, and laughter so bright.
The joy we discover, in moments so small,
It's the gift that keeps giving, the best one of all.

Cocoa and Comfort

Warm mugs in hand, we sip and we sigh,
With marshmallows floating, oh what a high!
Cups clink like bells, our cheers fill the room,
The cocoa's so rich, it can banish the gloom.

Blankets are piled, a soft cuddly nest,
As we bicker on who gets to sit best.
The cat claims the corner, with a haughty meow,
While we giggle and argue, over who has the wow.

Stories are shared, of trips gone awry,
Of failed holiday plans that made us all cry.
We laugh till we're sore, as we pass round the snacks,
Each munch a reminder, of our love that won't crack.

It's the simple delights that brighten our days,
With cocoa and laughter guiding our ways.
So lift up your mugs, let's cheer to the fun,
In this cozy little corner, we're all number one.

Hearthside Stories and Warmth

By the fire, tales unfold,
Of socks misplaced and cookies sold.
Grandpa's snore, a rhythmic beat,
While Auntie dances on her feet.

Mugs clink loudly in the light,
As pets plot mischief, quite a sight.
The cat steals ham, the dog looks shy,
Oh, the chaos is a joyful sigh!

Uncle Joe's jokes may fall quite flat,
But laughter's the warmest welcome mat.
We gather 'round in cozy cheer,
As winter's chill disappears, oh dear!

With playful banter, hearts ignite,
In this whimsical, joyful night.
Each story wrapped in snuggly glee,
A celebration meant to be!

Sweet Nothings Beneath the Stars

Under twinkling stars so bright,
Whispers float into the night.
Wishes made on candy canes,
As laughter dances, joy remains.

Snowflakes tumble, we all fall down,
Face plants cause a silly frown.
Friends make snowmen full of cheer,
Complete with hats, so jolly dear!

Hot cocoa spills, and marshmallows fly,
We end up giggling 'til we cry.
Tangled lights on a tree outside,
A festive whirlwind, a merry ride!

With sweet nothings, hearts align,
In frost-soaked moments, all is fine.
Beneath the stars, we take our stand,
Creating laughter, hand in hand.

Treading on a Path of Kindness

With every step, we laugh and play,
Leaving footprints of joy each day.
A neighbor's pie, a surprise delight,
Gifts exchanged in the morning light.

Dog on a leash, it pulls with glee,
While I trip over a gnarled tree.
Yet kindness blooms from every fall,
A lopsided grin conquers all!

We share our stories, some quite bizarre,
Like Auntie's sledding mishap in the car.
But with every mishap, love does grow,
On this wobbly path where laughter flows!

Treading lightly, our hearts embrace,
Living in joy, no time to waste.
With each cheerful step, we forge a way,
Building a world where kindness stays!

A Symphony of Hope and Harmony

In a quirky choir, we all partake,
Singing off-key for laughter's sake.
Jingle bells ring, out of tune,
But spirits soar, like a bright balloon!

With pots and pans, we drum along,
An orchestra of a clumsy song.
Mom's pasta bends, and sauce goes flying,
Yet in this chaos, nobody's crying!

Fuzzy socks and mismatched wear,
Uncle's dance moves, a sight too rare.
Harmony found in giggles bright,
As joy fills every nook, delight!

A symphony built on laughter's beat,
Creating memories, oh so sweet.
When love plays on, we all belong,
In this merry heartwarming song!